36 MILES OF TROUBLE

NORTHBOUND TRAIN AT THREE BRIDGES, BRATTLEBORO

36 MILES OF TROUBLE

The Story of the West River RR

by VICTOR MORSE

SHORTLINE RR SERIES

BRATTLEBORO * * * * * * * THE STEPHEN GREENE PRESS

		52	50	Mls	BRATTLEBORO AND SOUTH LONDONDERRY. *December* 31, 1905.	53	51		
....	....	Noon	A M		....LEAVE]	A M	P M	....	....
....	....	†1215	†7 00	0	+.**South Londonderry**.ᶞ	11 50	8 00	....	....
....	....	12 35	7 10	4	..........Winhall............	11 20	7 45	....	....
....	....	1 05	7 25	9	..........Jamaica..........ᶞ	10 50	7 25	....	....
....	....	1 30	7 35	13	.........Wardsboro.........	10 25	7 10	....	....
....	....	1 40	7 38	14	....West Townshend......	10 15	7 05	....	....
....	....	2 10	7 53	19	........Townshend........	9 45	6 45	....	....
....	....	2 45	8 08	23	+........Newfane........ᶞ	9 20	6 30	....	....
....	....	3 10	8 20	26	......Williamsville......	9 00	6 20	....	....
....	....	3 35	8 30	29	.....West Dummerston.....	8 30	6 10	....	....
....	....	4 15	8 55	36	+.....**Brattleboro**.....ᶞ	†7 50	†5 45	....	....
....	....	P M	A M		ARRIVE]	A M	P M	....	....

*Daily; †daily, except Sunday. + Coupon stations; ᶞ Telegraph stations.

REVISED EDITION
First edition published 1959, reprinted 1960, 1961, 1964, 1966.

73 74 75 76 77 78 79 9 8 7 6 5 4 3 2 1

ACKNOWLEDGEMENTS
and Photo Credits

The author is grateful to Mr. Lewis R. Brown of Brattleboro, Vermont, for useful suggestions and for permission to reproduce the photographs on pages 11, 16, 20, 23, 30, 32, 35, and 41; to Mr. Jason E. Bushnell for the photograph on page 9; to the New York Historical Society for the Lucius H. Tatham frontispiece photograph from the collection of Mrs. T. K. Boardman, Jr.; to the *Brattleboro Daily Reformer* for the photograph on page 19.

In the preparation of the Revised Edition special thanks are due to Mr. Robert L. Crowell for generously allowing access to his collection of West River RR memorabilia, from which come the timetable and map on the title page, and photographs as follows: unknown photographers, pages 17 and 26; John Dale, from the collection of the late Norman Hunt, page 36; Porter C. Thayer, engine No. 192 and train, above, and others on pages 22, 37 and 43, all reproduced by permission of Mrs. Porter C. Thayer. Aldren A. Watson contributed the drawing decorating the half-title and pages 1 and 3 following.

FOREWORD

This account was originally written for, and run serially in, the *Brattleboro Daily Reformer* to encourage sale of the newspaper, which it did. Later it was reprinted as a pamphlet, neither copyrighted nor reviewed, and was sold on retail stands in the neighborhood. A continuing demand for copies has prompted this new edition which requires the same sort of courage as did the building of the line.

Vestiges of the railroad grow steadily rarer. They have persisted best north of Jamaica village where the railroad followed the river around the east side of Ball Mountain while the highway climbed over the west shoulder. The old roadbed has been used by motor traffic ever since the rails came up, and it gives access to some good trout fishing and some dandy places for unadorned swimming. Camps were built along the way, too. In this seven-mile stretch through forest land the railroad crossed the river once, at Pratt Bridge. In World War II scrap iron became dear enough to make this span worth money and it was advertised for sale by the State of Vermont, the owner. But pressure from sportsmen was too great—Pratt Bridge did not go to war.

The flood control dam now a-building against Ball Mountain will make all this different.

In places where the railroad intersected the highway well-worn wheel tracks, vanishing into the forest, show where autos continue to use the route of the Bull of the Woods, as the train was un-affectionately known to railroad men. Between Newfane and Townshend, State Route No. 30 runs hard by abutments of the Salmon Hole Bridge, an enduring monument to legislative generosity.

A substantial part of the roadbed can be driven over, the ties so well-rotted that the way is now smooth. Heavy trucks used it for a mile or two north from the mouth of West River to carry concrete to a huge bridge on four-lane Interstate Highway No. 91. In Newfane is a stretch with two lines of cattle fence—one built by the railroad and the other, closer to the track, strung up by a land-hungry farmer—when the railroad ceased to maintain one.

I earned college money on the West River line one summer—the summer they rebuilt it with state money. I had had a couple of summers' experience "out on the main line" and they quickly chose me timekeeper from a motley crew of transients that answered the call for labor. There were more men than tools and in a day or two the chief engineer fired half of them. They converged on me demanding their pay and, in the absence of instructions, I tore up some paper bags and wrote them out orders on the railroad's treasurer. These they took to Brattleboro and, finding no treasurer, presented them at the Brattleboro Trust Company, which began honoring them. Somebody soon put a stop to this.

In general, people everywhere react alike, and by changing the names you could make this the story of any number of backwater railroads, including some of the Old Colony segments which Massachusetts politicians are now wringing the last capital out of—political capital, that is. The hard capital was gone long ago. At present, I make crossties for the Bangor & Aroostook, the only New England railroad earning any money to buy them with.

Brattleboro, 1959   VICTOR MORSE

2

36 MILES OF TROUBLE

To ACCUSE VERMONT'S WEST RIVER RAILROAD of being a complete failure would be doing it an injustice. It had its merits, though its faults were more numerous and more obvious. Neither could it be called an unqualified success for even the briefest part of its fifty-six-year history without torturing the record.

The railroad resulted from the valley's desire for one, a desire so fervent that it was subsidized readily and heavily. In return the people of the valley got its social benefits and on the whole were well satisfied. Of economic benefits there was none and, if any was expected, most people accepted the disappointment gracefully.

As a matter of cold economic fact it was money wasted. Indeed the 36-mile line never paid its way and the return to the original stockholders was negligible. While some of the valley's residents disputed the Central Vermont's system of bookkeeping which consistently showed annual deficits, nobody could ever find where the CV was reaping a harvest. In the end they took a turn at running it and found out for themselves.

Nor did it ever contribute to the prosperity of the towns it served. It added nothing to their little industries and gave them no new ones. It made their farms no more profitable. In short it brought the valley no extra business at all, except for transient lumbering which may or may not have been facilitated. There is no more eloquent testimony on this point than the census figures. All the towns lost population just as steadily after the railroad was built as in the three decades before.

But the value of a transportation system is not calculated on ledgers alone. Social benefits may justify it and the valley folk for the most part prefer to think this was the case with their railroad. It cut the trip from South Londonderry to Brattleboro from two days to two hours (if the train didn't break down) and brought all the valley towns closer together. Certainly they would never have known the Valley Fair and other flesh-pots of Brattleboro so intimately or in such numbers without the railroad.

The West River Railroad had its genesis in the movement to connect the Champlain and Connecticut valleys back before the Civil War. In 1843 the Vermont legislature granted a charter for the Champlain & Connecticut River Valley Railroad to run from Burlington to some point in Windham or Windsor County. New Hampshire was not granting railroad charters at that time and the plan was for the Boston-Fitchburg (Massachusetts) line to be extended to Brattleboro. From Brattleboro a railroad was to run up the West River Valley, cross the Green Mountains at East Wallingford and strike the present Rutland-Bellows Falls line. This route was actually surveyed and a half-mile tunnel was planned to run under the mountains in Weston.

Before this scheme got further New Hampshire permitted construction of a railroad from Fitchburg to Bellows Falls and the present Rutland Railroad was built to connect the latter with Burlington by way of Rutland.

In 1851 West River visionaries got another charter, this time for the Wantastiquet Railroad Company to run from Brattleboro up the valley through Londonderry, Landgrove and Peru to connect with the Western Vermont (now part of the Rutland) at some point in Danby or Wallingford. No further action was ever taken by this company.

For several years the railroad project lay dormant but the valley was not ready to relinquish its dream. This, let it be remembered, was the age when railroads were grinding out profits at every turn of the wheel, when the Union Pacific was being thrown across the continent and when the railroad barons were mulcting the federal government by that great swindle, the Credit Mobilier. Jay Gould and Brattleboro's own Jim Fisk were showing the rest how to water railroad stock by their manipulations of the Erie, and the ribbons of iron were spreading out to every sizable community in the land. Railroad operators made or broke industries, depending on whether they decided to give them a siding. Goods flowed in a never-ending stream into the great markets of the world and every business not on a railroad saw the hopelessness of trying to compete.

The result was a railroad fever that infected the entire nation. Every town wanted a railroad, and where private capital couldn't be interested municipal treasuries were tapped. To cut construction costs the narrow gauge, now little more than a memory, was conceived. Stock was subscribed in community campaigns and estimates of profit were lavish.

In this state of affairs the legislature gave the West River project a fresh push in 1867 by chartering the West River Railroad Company to build a line from Brattleboro to Jamaica but refused to let the towns go into debt to finance it. The following year it removed this obstacle and Jamaica, Townshend and Newfane promptly voted to bond themselves

SOUTH LONDONDERRY

Windham   *Grafton*   Saxtons

WINHALL

WINDHAM   GRAFTON

WSONVILLE

S Windham   Saxtons

Ball
Mountain   ATHENS

JAMAICA   ATHENS   WE

MAICA   E Jamaica   WEST TOWNSHEND
WARDSBORO (Sta.)   TOWNSHEND

MAICA   West   TOWNSHEND

DSBORO   *Wardsboro*   River   BROOKLINE   PUTNEY

WARDSBORO CEN.   West River   RR

DSBORO   Salmon
Hole   PUT

S Wardsboro   BROOKLINE

NEWFANE

NEWFANE

ER   E Dover   DOVER   WILLIAMSVILLE   *Dummerston*
                                                              EL

DOVER   Rock River   (Sta.)

Newfane

Route of the West River RR

River and rail line have been exaggerated against the background of a contemporary map prepared and copyright by The National Survey, Chester, Vermont 05413, and used by permission.

WEST DUMMERSTON   DUMMERSTON
                                            DUMMERSTON
                                            (Sta.)

BRATTLEBORO

MARLBORO   Three Bridges   Conn. R

Marlboro

W Brattlebor   BRATTLEBORO

eight times their grand lists, or 8 percent of the tax valuation of all their taxable property. In 1870 the corporation was formally organized but no capital was in sight beyond that offered by the three towns, and in 1872 the legislature was persuaded to extend for ten years the time in which the road might be completed. The next year a route to Jamaica was surveyed but nothing more was done until 1876.

Meanwhile narrow-gauge railroads rose in favor, being less expensive to build than those of standard width (56½ inches) and being more or less satisfactory for light traffic. Friends of the West River, failing to interest enough private capital to make a standard-gauge railroad possible, conceived a 3-foot line and an extension to Whitehall, New York. The legislature approved, transferred the West River's rights to the Brattleboro & Whitehall, and efforts to raise the money were renewed.

Whitehall capitalists professed great interest, as did all the towns along the route, but the vital spark still burned only in the West River Valley. By the spring of 1877 Brattleboro and Londonderry had voted to bond, adding their support to the three towns which had so voted earlier, but communities on the west side of the mountains failed to do so and the project slowed to a standstill again.

Soon word came of construction of a 2-foot line, reputed to be inexpensive and an unqualified success, from Bedford to Billerica, Massachusetts. Here valley proponents saw a chance to go ahead with their end of the railroad without help from across the mountains and a party of thirty promptly went to Billerica. They came home enthusiastic and duplication was warmly endorsed. Aid voted to a 3-foot line was transferred to a 2-foot one with the understanding that no vote would be valid until $200,000 had been raised. The towns bonded as follows:

Brattleboro	$ 50,000
Newfane	25,000
Townshend	37,000
Jamaica	32,800
Londonderry	23,000
	$167,800

This money bought common stock and the balance of the $200,000 was raised by private subscription, the last share being subscribed in Townshend in May, 1878. The rest of the cost, an estimated $350,000, was to be met by a bond issue.

A complete survey was made at once and in October the contract was let to Harris Brothers & Company for construction and equipment. Finally, 3-foot gauge was decided on.

6

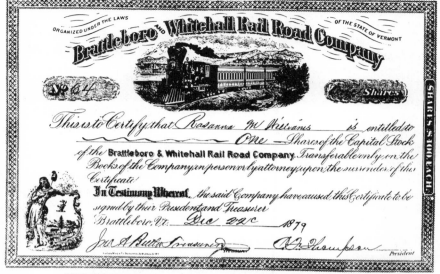

THIS CERTIFICATE WAS NEVER WORTH MORE THAN IN 1879

Hopes of the promoters were bright, to say the least. The stock prospectus estimated operating expenses and revenues in detail and forecast annual net income of $30,000. This, it was pointed out, was on local business alone and would be dwarfed by profits from through traffic when the line was extended to Whitehall. The extension was called certain within a few years and the B&W—Brattleboro & Whitehall—was to become the main route of transportation between the Champlain valley and the Atlantic seaboard. Further, with the aid of the Erie Canal and others to be built, it was to be a link in a rail-water system extending to the Great Lakes. Before many years the futility of this dream was more apparent, but had the promoters been less enthusiastic the railroad might never have reached even South Londonderry.

On November 11, 1878, ground was formally broken at Newfane amid oratory, fanfare and prayer, the last proving to be what was needed most. Officers of the company and prominent citizens made speeches after which the first president, C. F. Thompson, tossed aside a shovelful of earth. Wildly enthusiastic, the crowd followed his example, one after another. Old and young, lame and infirm, men and women—all stepped forward to throw dirt in the air. Even some implacable opponents were carried away and joined the shoveling fest.

Whatever honor there was in breaking the sod actually went to Jamaica, which got so excited that it held a ceremony of its own a few hours earlier the same day. There were speech-making, music by the Jamaica cornet band, firing of guns, ringing of bells and other symbols of community joy. Jamaica, incidentally, was the last town to clear its railroad debt. The final bond was paid in 1929, fifty years after the first train ran and six years before the rails were torn up.

The following spring found construction at full speed, but by July financial difficulties were in sight. Nevertheless, the roadbed was pushed to completion; and in the fall the treasury ran dry without a single rail laid. During the winter the company took the only convenient way out, which was to give the railroad to the Central Vermont to complete by spending $150,000 more.

In its lease the CV agreed to keep the line in repair, run at least two trains each way daily, divide all profits equally with the B&W and pay the B&W $400 a year to sustain its corporate existence (this was paid religiously until a different arrangement was made). But the CV never reported any profit to divide, and the $150,000 spent to finish the road became a first mortgage.

Evidently the railroad was worth fighting over in those days, if it could be had for $150,000. The B&W had leased a strip of land from the Vermont Valley to enter Brattleboro, but soon after the CV gained control the Vermont Valley tracks were thrown over on the B&W's right of way.

This strip ran from the Three Bridges southward about a mile to Brattleboro station and there was no other way for the B&W to enter Brattleboro or to connect with the Central Vermont tracks. The Vermont Valley, later absorbed into the Boston & Maine system, announced that the CV would not be permitted to join the B&W over its land without making "an arrangement," and the matter was promptly headed for the courts.

The litigation was short-lived. The Vermont Valley was ordered to return its tracks to its own roadbed and also lost its plea to have the CV's lease set aside.

With this hassle out of the way, construction went swiftly forward and on October 20, 1880, the last rail was laid without fanfare near the northern terminus, South Londonderry. For a fortnight ballasting and other refinements continued and on November 4 the first passenger train to travel the whole distance carried B&W and CV officials on an informal opening. On November 18 the public got its chance to ride, and the first regular train puffed from South Londonderry to Brattleboro through clusters of waving, gaping onlookers.

At last the railroad had come and joy reigned throughout the valley. Even the irreconcilable opponents, of whom there were a few in every town and who vigorously contended the railroad was utterly impractical, had to content themselves with saying the thing wasn't safe to ride on. The first equipment seemed lavish and the *Vermont Phoenix*, the local weekly newspaper, proudly reported that it consisted of two locomotives, the *Brattleboro* and the *Londonderry*, two combination baggage-passenger cars, two "observation" (slightly refined passenger) cars, fifteen flatcars and fifteen boxcars. Subsequently the rolling stock was increased.

The West River Railroad's best years were its first. In the two decades before the turn of the century it enjoyed its greatest patronage, which was

NORTHERN TERMINUS OF THE LINE: SOUTH LONDONDERRY STATION

nothing to rejoice about, and gave its best service, which was nothing to excite praise. It did, however, achieve a settled condition after the humps in the roadbed were ironed out and ledges overhanging in the path of the locomotives were cleared away; then trains plied the valley with more or less regularity.

By June, 1881, there was enough business so that a third wood-burning locomotive, the *J. L. Martin,* named in honor of the Brattleboro man who labored so hard to make the railroad a reality, was added. An average of twelve hundred passengers a month was reported for the first six months, but this was not up to expectations because many persons were still afraid to ride on it.

The situation moved the local weekly to declare that it was "a matter of ordinary prudence for the people of Brattleboro to not only drop all silly

9

clamor about the road not being safe, but to take hold and help make it the success and adjunct to our business which it may readily be made to be." Evidently the doubtful were gradually reassured, for ticket sales improved and at the end of the year twenty-three thousand had been sold.

From that first year forward the valley accepted the railroad and soon the Central Vermont was advertising round-trip tickets from South Londonderry to the G. A. R. encampment at Washington for $11.50.

Busy days found three-car passenger trains packed and sometimes one hundred fifty to two hundred tickets were sold at South Londonderry. Likewise express business boomed and frequently as much as seven tons was brought into Brattleboro. The mixed train hauled from fifteen to twenty-five freight cars and sometimes a coach full of passengers who idled their time away as the train, stopping at every other siding to set off and pick up cars, inched its way along.

Traditionally the biggest days were those of Brattleboro's Valley Fair. The entire valley, or as much of it as two locomotives could haul, turned out, and all rules were cast aside. Every piece of rolling stock was commandeered (since it was a narrow-gauge line none could be imported from other railroads) and was seldom enough. Before the train pulled out of South Londonderry all the passenger coaches were crammed and passengers down the line had the comforts of crude plank benches set in boxcars. At that, by the time the train got to Brattleboro, some were sitting on top of the cars, hanging on the sides and bulging out the doors. The railroad company always had an army of conductors on hand and it is said that fares were collected from almost everybody.

At night, those who hoped to have a seat for the ride home were at the Brattleboro depot hours ahead of time, standing in line until the cars were brought to the platform. Once when the crowd was extraordinary, even for Fair Day, rain started and there was a stampede for the shelter of the platform roof, far from adequate. One woman fainted. Another pulled out her hat pin and began jabbing those pushing behind her, who were being pushed themselves. It took the police department to quell the disorder.

Even the best passenger cars were small and stuffy and the boxcars worse. A throng of weary, jaded passengers found the ride home a tedious ordeal but to go to Brattleboro's fair was a rare treat. Up and down the valley today are graying oldsters who can remember the thrill they had as half-scared youngsters.

Second to the fair ran the annual stockholders' meeting, the main feature of which was a free dinner in a Brattleboro hotel. The shares were transferable and anyone who presented a certificate to the conductor on annual meeting day had a free ride. A share was likewise a dinner ticket, and

10

everybody who could beg one was in the crowd. Many families had five or ten shares or more, so they turned out in full strength along with their cousins. About three hundred shares were privately held and few of them were not represented at the dinner. The other seventeen hundred were held by the towns, and by various acts of official legerdemain these got into numerous hands.

But for all the patronage the West River had on occasion, the profits consistently failed to appear. Every year the Central Vermont turned $400 into the B&W treasury, but nothing else. The stockholders' dinner was the B&W's sole expense and always left a respectable balance of the $400, so as often as $2,000 accumulated a 1 percent dividend was paid. This, distributed about half a dozen times, was all the stockholders ever got.

Quickly the railroad became a community fixture. It was seldom spoken of as the Brattleboro & Whitehall, or the Central Vermont, or the West River, which finally became its corporate name. Instead it was "the narrow gauge," which before long was shortened to "the gauge." Even after it was widened to standard gauge it was still "the gauge" and gradually the valley it served came to be known loosely by the same name. To this day a trip up the valley is often called "going up the gauge."

Toward the end of its narrow-gauge days the railroad boasted a coal-burning locomotive which the CV picked off a scrap heap somwhere, but most of the traffic was hauled by the three wood-burners. The tenders

ENGINE NO. 2, NARROW-GAUGE WOOD BURNER, 1879-1905

11

carried a couple of cords of chunks and at intervals along the line were big woodpiles for refueling. If the train crew alone had the job of "wooding up" it took half an hour, but the time was rare when the male passengers didn't lend a hand. With a crowd of men and boys throwing on chunks the delay was cut to ten minutes and the passengers, with a wearying journey ahead of them, were glad enough to save the time.

When Levi Fuller was governor he once went to South Londonderry for the week-end and when he started back he joined the rest at the woodpile. He took a position near the tender and every time he straightened up his beaver hat hit it and was knocked to the ground. He gave the hat to a crew member to hold while he pitched on his share.

Before long the railroad also became locally notorious for delay, although it was never as bad as the wits painted it. True, passengers often got off to pick berries or flowers or visit with farmers, but such stories originated mostly from the mixed train that also hauled freight. At every station the crew had to unload freight, shift boxcars and so on; and since it might be a matter of half an hour the passengers in the tail-end coach amused themselves as best they could. The conductor was faithful about rounding them up when it was time to go along.

Waits were also common at the foot of the hills on either side of Newfane. Frequently the engine could only pull up half the train at a time, so it would have to put one section on the Newfane siding and go back for the other. One trainman was said to leave the train when the first section got to Newfane to pay a half-hour's court to a widow. At Williamsville station the crew also took the time to pass around water from a cold spring.

In deer season the crew, and sometimes the passengers, carried rifles in case a buck came into view. More than once the train was stopped for a volley and the railroad carried a lot of venison without bills of lading.

Probably the most famous unbilled shipment was a calf which arrived in Newfane in a car containing only a cow when it started. There was a bill of lading for the cow but not the calf, so the station agent promptly wired headquarters for instructions. Should he hold the calf until the farmer paid freight on it? Soon CV files contained a voluminous folder of enlightening and entertaining correspondence on the subject but the farmer got his calf before the railroad wits had worn the topic out.

If the railroad had boasted as many passengers as spectators its finances might have been another story. From the first the most popular summer evening diversion in valley villages was to go to the station to watch the train come in. The practice continued almost to the railroad's last days and at such stations as Newfane, Townshend and Jamaica there were often one hundred or more on hand. As years wore on and the motive power grew feeble with age the wait often was a long one. Postmasters and towns-people who expected a letter fretted, for the train also brought the mail, and on such occasions the hoarse whistle of the Bull of the Woods brought a mixture of thrill and relief.

Newfane got an advance warning when the train whistled for a crossing below the village and this whistle was a signal for the two innkeepers to run to the station to gather whatever patronage might alight. In the course of time a Newfane lad taught himself to emit a good imitation of the loco-motive's shriek and, on cold winter nights about twenty minutes before train time, would let out a blast outside one of the hotels. That innkeeper stood around in the cold alone a lot of times.

Unreliable as West River trains came to be, it was never strictly true that they would wait at a station for a hen to lay another egg so the farmer would have a dozen to send to Brattleboro. As often as not, however, the hen had plenty of time.

The story is also told of a Jamaica man who wanted to go to Brattleboro when the mixed train arrived about noon but didn't want to start without his dinner. He took the conductor home to eat with him and the train waited. This has never been substantiated, nor has the yarn about the woman who started for Brattleboro for her confinement but had her baby before the train got there. In the same class is the man who lost his false teeth while leaning out the window. According to legend the conductor stopped the train while all the passengers got out to hunt. They found the teeth.

To get the railroad built at all the contractors had to overlook fine points and the shortcomings of its construction plagued it almost to its dying day. No money was wasted making the roadbed an inch wider than necessary or cutting away any ledges that could be left. The track didn't have any ballast that it could get along without, and in a lot of places didn't have as much as it needed. For much of the distance the roadbed was a narrow path cut in the side of ledges, and when the locomotive started swaying, as it was apt to do when it got up to twenty-five miles an hour, it would bump into projecting rock. More than once it limped home with some more or less vital part knocked off in this manner. In the course of time this process wore the biggest projections off the ledges and less trouble was experienced.

Bridges were likewise slighted in construction and promptly began to collapse under spring and fall freshets until, by the turn of the century, every major bridge had been replaced. The first ones were built of wood, hardly strong enough for the strain, far from durable and always at the mercy of high water. As they went they were replaced with wide, relatively

LUCKY COLLAPSE OF THE TRESTLE (LEFT) KEPT THE DEATH TOLL TO TWO IN THIS 1886 WRECK

sturdy iron bridges, which by 1892 caused the local papers to predict the change to standard gauge.

First and most disastrous of the bridge losses was the collapse in 1886 of the bridge across the mouth of West River near Brattleboro under the weight of the mixed train. The accident took two lives.

As the train rolled onto it, the main span splintered and crumbled with a roar and bridge, engine and seven freight cars plunged in a tangled mass to the river bottom forty feet below. Not a match stick was left between the abutments. The first span carried the track over the sloping riverbank and by some stroke of fortune this collapsed too, letting the passenger car with thirteen persons aboard down on dry land. J. J. Green, Newfane station agent, was killed in the car's fall and five others were badly hurt. The engineer, H. A. Smith, died under water, pinned in his cab. Two others, the fireman and a brakeman, were carried into the river but swam ashore. Had not the approach span collapsed the passenger car would have rolled off the abutment into the river.

The crash was heard for a mile and witnesses said the entire bridge went down at once. Engineers never explained the accident but self-appointed investigators had much to say about pieces of rotten wood they picked up. Immediately a $15,000 iron bridge was built, and to reassure the public it was tested with ten flatcars each carrying twenty tons of Dummerston granite. Meanwhile, the bridge was the railroad's southern terminal for a year, and teams supplied the connecting link to Brattleboro.

In 1887 the Salmon Hole bridge north of Newfane was destroyed by fire and a year thereafter a second wooden one was carried out by ice. A third was badly damaged a few years later and the iron bridge built in its place stood until the flood of 1927. Flood reconstruction brought a fifth. In the early years the railroad was too important for a suspension of traffic while a bridge was being built, so trains ran up to each bank of the river and passengers and freight were ferried across.

One day toward the end of the century a train left Brattleboro but stopped at the West Dummerston bridge when the engineer saw it swaying and trembling under the impact of flood waters. Soon the southbound train reached the other end and passengers walked across. H. G. Barber crossed two minutes before the bridge went out. E. L. Hastings was still on when it sank but he leaped to safety. At the time a new iron bridge was nearing completion alongside.

High water took its toll of the roadbed too, and hardly a spring or fall passed that traffic wasn't suspended by washouts. A small trestle at West Townshend acquired an almost annual habit of being washed away, the high bank above Jamaica slid into the track after almost every hard rain, and the track near Brattleboro was left dangling in the air at frequent intervals.

In 1896 a rather serious spring freshet caused washouts at Brattleboro and Townshend, tore out two trestles and left a landslide fifteen feet deep on a section of the track north of Townshend. A train started from South Londonderry on a Monday morning when the freshet was at its height, got no farther than Wardsboro, and five days later its mail came into Brattleboro on a handcar. Passengers waited in Brattleboro from Monday until Thursday, when a train took them to Townshend. Teams carried them to another at Wardsboro.

When a spring flood swept away about five hundred feet of low trestle north of Wardsboro Station, transfer around the gap by teams was necessary for several days. An engine and a lone car were used on the South Londonderry end and one morning started down with six passengers, a pile of lumber and a calf. Out of the incident grew this ballad, which was resurrected and included in VERMONT FOLK SONGS AND BALLADS:

We've got a little railroad   We put in twenty thousand
And it isn't very wide.   And quite a lot beside.

THE *LONDONDERRY* HEADS OUT OF BRATTLEBORO ON DUAL GAUGE TRACK

CROSSING THE WEST RIVER AT WEST DUMMERSTON. LOCO NO. 36
IS PROBABLY ON THE HEAD END

They took all our money—
  It was something of a chunk;
It is now being run
  By the old Grand Trunk.

They started Monday morning
  At seven o'clock on time,
I say they had six passengers
  That were going down the line.
A sheriff and a parson,
  Three ladies, now don't laugh,
A little pile of lumber
  And a little red calf.

They had but one car
  For the whole blamed lot;
They hadn't any stove
  And it wasn't very hot;
They hadn't any seats
  So they were in sore distress;

They took the crowd along
  As baggage and express.

The sheriff, he looked wise,
  And the baggage master, too
The expressman, how he swore,
  As all expressmen do.
Captain Davis took the minister
  Most kindly in his charge,
He put him in the mail bag
  As he wasn't very large.

The conductor waved his hand
  And the calf began to bleat.
Then Bert, he pulled the throttle
  And the thing began to start.
They left the depot right on time,
  All in the same stall —
The parson and the sheriff,
  The lumber, calf and all.

At another time the august judge of Windham County court, his retinue, lawyers, plaintiffs and defendants tramped through a long washout on the meadows north of Brattleboro to board a train waiting to take them to Newfane for the session's opening.

By 1898 several wooden bridges had been replaced by standard-gauge iron ones and the B&W stockholders at their annual meeting heard that the CV would replace the rest without waiting for them to be washed away. They also heard that steel rails had been laid in place of iron ones for half the distance and would go into South Londonderry the next year. Another projected improvement was replacement of rotten crossties which had been the subject of aroused comment the year before, and talk of broad gauge was rife. This was almost the last optimistic note struck in the railroad's history.

As early as 1895 signs of the railroad's disintegration were apparent. Crossties rotted and let rails spread out of line until trains went off the track with annoying frequency. The locomotives grew feeble and the cars rickety. There was little equipment except that bought when the line was opened and, as it deteriorated, scant attention was paid to repairs and less to replacement. Trains ran consistently late, mail was delayed and freight service was unpredictable.

By 1900 the service was a constant source of complaint and in the next few years became a point of increasing friction between the valley folk and the Central Vermont management.

A roundhouse fire at South Londonderry badly damaged one locomotive, the *J. L. Martin,* and destroyed the water tank. The tank wasn't replaced, and on every trip the crew had to fill the boiler with buckets. For a long time the railroad limped along with two locomotives. Finally the Central Vermont produced another aging contraption which languished on the hills.

The locomotive water tanks sprang leaks too, and sprayed water along the roadbed like sprinkling carts. Trains had to stop here and there while the crew shoveled in snow in winter and bailed water out of springs in summer. Woodpiles were allowed to become depleted and the local daily once charged that trees were felled along the way and stuffed into the firebox to keep steam up. According to the testimony of railroad veterans this was an exaggeration, but coal was shoveled into the woodburners in their last days when wood was scarce.

Passengers were held up hours at a time, sometimes midway between stations and far from habitation. Weary shoppers sat long after starting time waiting for the evening train to take them home from Brattleboro. These waits gave rise to the rumor that the train crew would get into a card game and not leave until someone had been fleeced; but it is more probable that they passed time with cards while they waited for the enginehouse mechanics to patch the motive power enough so it could get to South Londonderry.

On cold winter nights the little stoves which heated the passenger cars were stoked so vigorously they set the cars on fire. At other times they went out and left the passengers nearly freezing. Sometimes both happened on a single trip. One newspaper report told of a woman whose bouquet of flowers froze as she sat beside the stove.

"It (the railroad) has been a flat failure from the start," an editorial declared in 1903. "Today it is the most uncertain, the flimsiest, the most dangerous piece of public conveyance imaginable. . . . Nobody has ever been accused of failing to catch a train on this road. The meanest thing a passenger could do was drag his feet, for that brought it to a halt and stops were avoided if possible because of the uncertainty of the start. The timetable reads like a cookbook."

Even in South Londonderry, where the railroad's friends were to be found if it had any, the *Sifter* editorially remarked that the trains were run "try-daily, that is they went down in the morning and tried to get back at night."

A ROUTINE DERAILMENT ON THE OLD WEST RIVER RR

THE OLD *J. L. MARTIN* AT SO. LONDONDERRY, AND *(below)* NO. 320 FROM A LATER PERIOD

In this period the railroad's patrons pinned their best hopes on a change to broad gauge, often promised and almost given up when it at last came. First and loudest in demands for standard gauge was the Lyons Granite Company, which demanded a better outlet from its West Dummerston quarry. In 1901 the *Reformer* said the company had been obliged to turn away business and cut its force from one hundred and fifteen to thirty men because the railroad couldn't haul more than three cars of granite a day.

Not long afterward a third rail was laid from Brattleboro to West Dummerston so the track could accommodate both standard- and narrow-gauge trains, but that didn't diminish the complaints. The ties were so rotten the third rail wouldn't stay in place and continually let granite-laden cars down on the ground. Where it should have been curved it was straight and where it should have been straight it was curved, the newspaper said.

Steadily the chorus of complaints grew louder. At an indignation meeting called in Brattleboro the B&W directors heard a long line of shippers claim that service was inadequate, that lumber and goods stood beside the track waiting to be taken away, that mail often didn't arrive until postmasters had closed their offices and gone to bed. Station agents were said to be seventy-five to one hundred in arrears on orders for freight cars.

This state of affairs soon led to the courts. In 1903 the Brattleboro & Whitehall Company petitioned for receivership and asked that the lease be set aside. It claimed that the roadbed was unsafe, that the cars and locomotives were old, worn and unfit for service and that business along the line was suffering in consequence. The Central Vermont countered with a petition for foreclosure, alleging that the $150,000 mortgage was due. The line had never earned interest on the mortgage, the CV said, and in fact had been operated at a loss. Spokesmen for the CV publicly scoffed at a receivership, pointing out that the Brattleboro & Whitehall was without operating capital or credit, but CV meanwhile rushed in men and materials in an ineffective gesture toward repairs.

For nearly two years the litigation moldered in the courts and the railroad did the same in the valley. Finally, after protracted negotiations, the B&W agreed to consent to foreclosure and the CV to broad-gauge and repair the railroad. The CV also gave the B&W $5,000 to finance preservation of its corporate structure, extended passes to the directors and agreed to let stockholders ride free on annual meeting day for twenty years. The CV then organized the West River Railroad Company as nominal owner of the line and promptly put it $75,000 in debt to the parent company for broad-gauging. Of its promise to build a branch from Wardsboro Station through Stratton, Winhall and Peru to tap a rich lumber district, nothing more was heard.

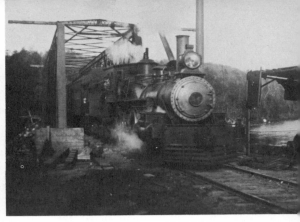

ENGINES NOS. 192 AND 54 DEMONSTRATE SOUTHBOUND ACTION IN NARROW-
AND BROAD-GAUGE VERSIONS OF ROCK RIVER BRIDGE

Immediately the roadbed was cleared and widened and new, longer ties were put in. On Sunday, July 30, 1905, the track was broad-gauged. Three hundred and fifty men, including every track crew between South Londonderry and New London, Connecticut and many from northern points toiled from daybreak until dark in pouring rain and threw one rail out to standard width all the way except for a mile. The job was completed the following morning.

The trip of the first broad-gauge train was reminiscent of the opening a quarter of a century earlier. All along the way the populace turned out for a gala day, while a big crowd gathered at Brattleboro to greet the train. The railroad began its new life with three locomotives and a small assortment of cars demoted from other parts of the CV system, and ever thereafter was a dumping ground for aging equipment.

The West River's new life on broad gauge soon proved to be less than had been hoped for. The track was widened and ballasted speedily but not carefully and often let the train down on the ground—sometimes, the paper reported, two or three times on a trip. Less than a month after the change the track sank from under a locomotive on Sand Hill south of Newfane and sent it hurtling down a fifty-foot bank. Engineer A. W. Shattuck was fatally scalded. His widow sued the CV and got a $6,000 verdict, although a brakeman who suffered a broken leg in a wreck two years later got $9,000.

In the next few months matters improved. Flaws left in broad-gauging were remedied and by the spring of 1906 service was reported much improved with prospect of restoration of the second daily passenger train. The extra train materialized but the railroad slipped back into its old habits.

For a railroad where a snail's pace was the rule and where two trains were seldom on the track at once, the West River had its share of accidents. Altogether it took five lives, all of them except that of Engineer Shattuck in its narrow-gauge days. When it was four years old it took its first in a wreck at the West Dummerston bridge. Just after the southbound mixed train got across the bridge, one car jumped off the track and the others toppled over like a row of dominoes. The passenger car and two boxcars rolled down the bank and one passenger, George Richmond of Jamaica, was killed. Seven of the fifteen others were hurt, three badly. A calf was dug out of a demolished box car unhurt.

In another fatal accident a section hand was killed. One afternoon the train rounded a curve near Brattleboro and came full upon a handcar bearing the section boss and his lone underling. The train was unable to stop because part of the braking mechanism had been broken by a protruding ledge, and James Caufield fell under the handcar trying to get it off the track. Several cars passed over him.

Two others died in the collapse of the Brattleboro Bridge and Shattuck's death completed the list. All except one were railroad employees.

Once the train struck an automobile on one of the numerous crossings north of Townshend, but without fatal results. All six occupants were hurt, two rather badly, and the car was demolished. One reason why the West River line, weaving back and forth across the highway most of the way, didn't have more crossing accidents may have been that, by the time automobiles came to be a serious problem, trains were few. At that, many were the times the engineer put on the brakes at the Three Bridges crossing above Brattleboro to keep out of a car's way. To do this irked the engineer, for he needed his speed to get over the grade and sometimes had to go back for another flying start.

On several occasions an engine or a car hopped off the iron and started

ENGINE NO. 54 NOSES INTO THE WEST RIVER NORTH OF JAMAICA

THE ENGINEER WAS BADLY HURT WHEN THE *LONDONDERRY* TURNED OVER

for the river but when anyone was injured it almost invariably was a railroad man. The passenger car usually was blessed with luck, although the occupants' thoughts flashed back over their sins when it began to bump along the ties. They were never certain whether it would tip over, plunge down a bank or shake to pieces.

One cold November day it tipped over above West Dummerston. In each end was a stove and these set the car afire. A great heap of mail bags went over, too, and Ernest J. Waterman was dragged from under them before the fire got to him. The rest crawled out—A. F. Schwenk with a sprained ankle—and eight or ten disgruntled passengers went back to Brattleboro in a boxcar.

Whatever trouble the railroad had from other sources, nothing made it more helpless than a blizzard. So often was the train stuck in snowdrifts that South Londonderry never bade it goodbye under a threatening winter sky without wondering when it would be seen again. Sometimes it was missing for days.

One March evening in 1887 three coaches laden with men and women who had spent the day at a Brattleboro horse show started back up the valley as a blizzard began. The wood-burner *Londonderry* plowed through the mounting snow well enough as far as West Dummerston, but there it stuck its cowcatcher into a drift and came peacefully to a stop. Nothing would make it go on, so the village was combed for accommodations. The hotel it then boasted took in eight women but a great many more and the men spent a relatively merry night in the cars waiting for the *J. L. Martin* to arrive from Brattleboro with a snowplow.

They were all still waiting the following morning, Sunday, so everybody went to church. About noon the *J. L. Martin* and the plow arrived, but even with this aid the train was soon stuck again. With the passengers and crew shoveling the biggest drifts ahead, nightfall saw the train in Jamaica, a comparative metropolis where the hotel accommodated all the women; the men had the comforts of the coaches again. Late Monday morning they saw South Londondery.

More than once this happened, in both narrow- and standard-gauge days, and the best that can be said for the railroad is that such incidents seldom happened twice in the same winter. At other times the engines stayed snug in the roundhouse until a storm blew itself out, which was fortunate for the passengers if they weren't on the wrong end of the line. Once a big crowd from various stations was waiting at Brattleboro on a stormy night when word went out that the train wouldn't leave. It was two days later when they started home, but Brattleboro hotels were at least more comfortable than the cars and the meals were served more regularly. In such cases the railroad company paid the hotel bills and light-hearted passengers made a lark of it. A wag once remarked that the only reason Newfane had two hotels was to take care of stranded trains. The Jamaica hotel also owed a lot of its business to the railroad.

In winter it was unfortunate that the hotels were not closer together, for the locomotives often took a notion to go to sleep midway between towns. Such was the case one day in March, 1900. A train which left here in the morning wasn't heard from after it left Townshend. Later in the day another, sent to its rescue, came upon it buried in ten-foot drifts below Jamaica. Both spent the night there and the next day passengers and crew shoveled the train's way into Jamaica. That night they slept in the hotel and the next day made South Londonderry.

Another time it took three locomotives, two snowplows, three train crews and two days to get four passengers from Brattleboro to South Londonderry. The four left on a regular train on a Tuesday afternoon. Until midnight the engine plowed through mounting snow but above Jamaica it nosed into a drift and stalled. The crew got word back to Brattleboro, and at 1:30 A.M. Wednesday another engine started to its relief with a snowplow. Near Williamsville Station the plow ran off the track, dived into a bank and wrecked itself.

At noon Wednesday a second relief engine left Brattleboro with a plow, picked up the other and its crew at Williamsville and managed to reach the stalled train near midnight. With three locomotives and plenty of shoveling, the four passengers got to South Londonderry Thursday noon.

Worst of all was the blizzard of '88, which engulfed two trains for eight days. A mixed train which left South Londonderry on a Monday and was snowed in half a mile above Jamaica got to Brattleboro on Tuesday of the

SUPERB OLD-TIME PHOTO OF AN EARLY WEST RIVER RR WRECK. PLACE, DATE AND—ALAS—THE PHOTOGRAPHER ARE UNKNOWN.

26

next week. A relief train spent the intervening time rescuing it.

The relief engine left Brattleboro with a snowplow early Monday afternoon and at nightfall had made Williamsville. The crew of seven elected to spend the night there, and three of their number went to a farmhouse half a mile away for food. They were five hours getting there and back and had to dig snow from the door to get in.

Daybreak revealed a locomotive almost completely buried. In all day it advanced little more than a mile, mainly by dint of shoveling. Tuesday night the crew stayed at a farmhouse and the next day developed a technique which brought Newfane almost within sight. The engine was driven full speed into drifts higher than its smokestack, shoveled out, backed up and driven in again.

Wednesday night the men went back to the same farmhouse and on Thursday, with fewer drifts to battle, got two miles beyond Townshend. They returned to Newfane for the night and on Friday reached the stalled mixed train. They found the cars hardly visible and only the smokestack of the locomotive showing above the snow. Passengers and crew had meanwhile reached Jamaica through the snow.

The mixed train was shoveled out and the two locomotives got behind the plow for a final push to South Londonderry. By this time the force of accompanying shovelers, augmented along the way and further reinforced by the mixed train's crew and passengers, had grown to thirty, and progress was rapid until Saturday when the plow went off the track and nearly slid into the river. One engine had to go back to Williamsville for tools and by the time the plow was back on the rails night had fallen. Late the next day, Sunday, South Londonderry was reached. On Monday morning the engines were turned around and started for Brattleboro with the mixed train. All went well until it reached Williamsville, where the track was badly drifted again. One engine dived off into a snowbank and spent most of the night there. Early Tuesday morning the train pulled into Brattleboro—thirty-six miles in eight days!

In all the times the train was marooned a day or more in snowdrifts there was no suffering. Somehow food was always found before anyone became desperately hungry; the cars were kept warm even if they didn't offer soft beds, and succor always came sooner or later.

The train crews grew accustomed to staying in the cars and soon learned what farmhouses could be relied upon to satisfy half a dozen hungry men. When farmhouses were not convenient (the tracks went through some long stretches of wilderness) there was always the express car, which carried large consignments of butter and eggs. A couple of dozen eggs could be

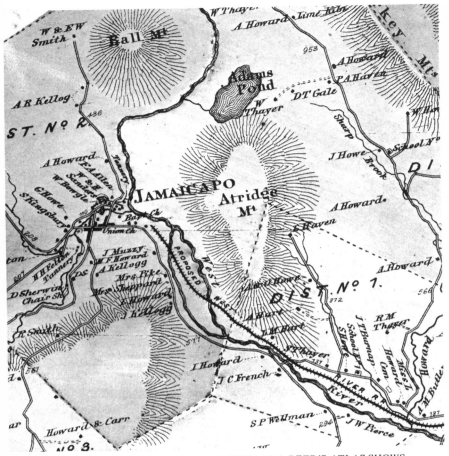

DETAIL OF RARE, HAND-COLORED MAP FROM 1869 *BEER'S ATLAS* SHOWS "PROPOSED WEST RIVER RR" TERMINATING AT JAMAICA, AS SPECIFIED IN THE 1867 CHARTER

put in a pail and hard-boiled quickly with steam from the engine's boiler. Sometimes a jug of cider would help them down. When the men tired of hard-boiled eggs they washed off a coal shovel and fried a few in the firebox. Passengers of a finicky nature had no trouble following the crew's lead when they got hungry enough.

Trainmen also learned to make light of putting the train back on the track and as a rule carried tools for the job. But hardened as they were, they got exasperated when the snowplow left the iron. Back in World War I a blizzard tied up the line a few days with trains stranded at Brattleboro and South Londonderry. When the storm cleared the Brattleboro crew took a plow and started to break out the track. The engine was puffing merrily along when a man looked out the caboose window and cried:

"What's that little house out on the river?"

The engineer knew, so he brought the train to a halt. It was the plow, with two men in it, which had jumped off the track, broken its coupling and slid out on the ice while the engine sailed along. The crew went back to Brattleboro for another plow and left that one for somebody else to get back on the iron.

By a stroke of fortune that the West River seldom enjoyed, no trains were caught in the longest tie-up on record. A foot of snow fell, a thaw turned it to slush and then the thermometer began to fall. Expecting trouble, the station agent at South Londonderry wired the CV division superintendent at New London, Connecticut, advising that the track be scraped.

"You run the South Londonderry station and I'll run the southern division," was the substance of the reply.

The track wasn't scraped, the slush froze and not a train ran for three weeks. When it was opened it was by an army of men with pickaxes. Meanwhile, four-horse teams transported mail and passengers from either end, meeting at Jamaica. The first mail to reach Brattleboro from South Londonderry bore a week-old postmark.

Within a year after the railroad was broad-gauged general debilitation set in again, partly due to the fact that the CV had an opportunity to equip it with rolling stock worn out elsewhere. Within two years patrons were complaining about the inadequacy of motive power. Of the three locomotives put on the line only one was in running order and the northbound train had to wait for the southbound to reach Brattleboro before it could start. Freight cars were scarce, too.

One December morning in 1907 the passenger train's engine broke down below West Townshend. A relief engine known as "the scrap heap" was sent up from Brattleboro but it, too, broke down short of Newfane. Meanwhile, a blizzard came out of the north and the thermometer fell. While passengers took turns warming themselves around a lone stove in one of the cars the conductor tramped to a telephone for aid. Hours dragged on and day turned to night, the passengers got colder and hungrier, but still no aid came.

At long last a third engine appeared and hauled the train to Newfane. The railroad might be crumbling to dust but nevertheless was run strictly according to the rules. The third engine had been sent out without any instructions about returning so the crew wired New London for further orders and stayed at Newfane. In an hour or so permission came to proceed

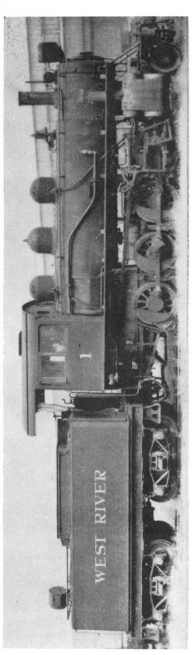

ENGINE NO. 1, $14,000 "PLANTATION" LOCOMOTIVE, WENT SOUTH AFTER ALL FOR $2,500

NO. 33 LEAVING SOUTH LONDONDERRY. STATION LIES BEHIND TRAIN; ENGINEHOUSE TO RIGHT OF WATER TOWER

and near midnight the train reached Brattleboro after thirteen hours on the road. Later it developed that while passengers sat in the cold, roundhouse mechanics at Brattleboro were rushing repairs on the third engine.

Breakdowns became increasingly common and passengers learned to while away their time waiting for another engine. By 1914 the *Reformer* was reporting such cases in these terms:

"No. 37, rated the best of the three antiquated pieces of alleged mechanism, to operate which a man must have an engineer's license and be a member of the Brotherhood, broke down this morning while trying to haul the two cars that comprise a train on the West River branch from South Londonderry to Brattleboro."

A month later the paper reported that the locomotives were patched almost daily, and at that, trains were consistently hours late and frequently stalled in the woods. "The whistle and bell are in good order," the editorial conceded.

One night thirty-four Brattleboro Odd Fellows had the temerity to charter a special train to attend a fraternal function in Wardsboro. They made the mistake of not starting home until 2 A.M. The train, which had to be divided and hauled up Newfane Hill a car at a time, reached Brattleboro at 5:10 A.M. "A record breaking run of twenty-three miles in three hours," said the paper.

Cars became as rickety as the engines. Two women who boarded the train at Williamsville in the middle of a rainstorm found water several inches deep on the car floor and had to sit with their feet up. The roof leaked so badly they also had to sit under their umbrellas and at that were soaked when they reached Brattleboro.

When it wasn't an ailing locomotive that caused delay it was derailment, a failing for which the mixed train became particularly noted. When the mixed ran light the engineer would yank open the throttle as he neared Salmon Hole bridge from the north so as to make the grade without dividing the train. Once when the clip was particularly fast the passenger car bobbed off the rails in the middle of the bridge and began to bump over the ties, shaking the liver out of the handful of passengers. There was no slackening of pace and the passengers and train crew, expecting to land in the river, started through the car in opposite directions and became a heap in the middle. At the end of the bridge the car jumped back on the track and the engineer didn't know it had been off until he was told.

A weary old man who boarded the mixed train was jolted awake with the car on its side at the bottom of a bank.

"What station is this?" he cried.

"It's an accident," yelled the brakeman from under a seat.

THIS SNOWPLOW LOST ITS WAY NEAR JAMAICA IN 1921

"Oh, I thought that was the way you always stopped."

Another time everything of the mixed train except the locomotive went off the iron at Townshend and some of the passengers rode into 'Derry on the cowcatcher. But that was a better day than the one that saw three trains go off in succession. Every bit of motive power the West River could muster was on the ground that time. For no particular reason the train most often derailed was the southbound mixed, usually between Newfane and Brattleboro. Many were the times passengers waiting here for the night train didn't get away until early morning or the next day.

Although most derailments occurred without obvious reason the night passenger train once had a good excuse. A bull which refused to yield the right of way put the engine off below Townshend, although the animal got cut in two for its pains.

With transportation in this condition a Wardsboro man who had a carload of cattle shipped from Essex Junction unloaded them at Putney and drove them to his farm over the roads. He said he would rather drive them than risk having them killed on the West River, and besides, it was quicker.

When the track was widened there were two trains, a mixed and a passenger, each way daily. In a few years the number was increased to three and then to four—or at least the timetable called for as many, although it often was the next day before the last had reached its terminal. In 1913 the first Sunday train ran, but only briefly. Thereafter the number declined along with patronage, although the valley fought each curtailment bitterly and retrenchment seldom came until it was long overdue. By 1920 passenger trains had disappeared altogether. After some urging the CV restored them three days a week, but with the condition that they also handle less than carload lots of perishable freight when necessary. Finally the passenger train was dropped for all time.

Early in the days when there was only the mixed train the timetable gave it a different number going up from what it had coming down. Thus, under the railroad regulations there were two entirely different trains, and one could not be on the track when the other was scheduled. The train going up would be so late that it wouldn't get to 'Derry by the time it was supposed to return, so it would take a sidetrack at Jamaica or some such place while the conductor telegraphed to New London for permission to proceed. After the matter had been carried high enough in the CV's official circles, the mixed got a special dispensation to run against itself.

One of the things with which the CV tried to solve the West River problem was an Edison storage battery electric car which was brought here in the summer of 1914 and given a few trials. The CV said it was a "revolution" in branch-line transportation and would give adequate service at low cost.

On its first regular trip it went off the iron, was hauled back in humiliation by a steam engine and didn't get out of the shop for two weeks. Later it ran satisfactorily as far as West Townshend and in the fall the CV, pronouncing it a success, said it would begin regular trips the following spring. It was never seen here again.

The West River's propensity for physical collapse, which made it a local laughingstock and exasperated those it pretended to serve, also made it one of the nation's most profitable lines for railroad workers. Overtime was the rule rather than the exception for train crews, and at time-and-a-half it netted some fat pay envelopes. Wages were the same as on main lines and men kept out half the night or more by an ailing locomotive were well paid for their trouble. Only once—when railroad men on the entire Grand Trunk system, of which the CV had become a part, struck for higher pay—did it suffer labor trouble. Along with the rest of the system it was tied up for two weeks in 1910 while the Brotherhoods were wringing out a raise.

The valley didn't take these growing physical shortcomings without a murmur. The broad gauge wasn't a year old when protests began to accumulate at St. Albans and by the time the 1927 flood all but wiped the railroad off the map, valley shippers had figuratively shouted themselves hoarse. Though they battled with increasing despair they kept it up until the end, meanwhile diverting more and more of their business to the highways.

Chief among the complainants were the lumbermen, for at that time forests in the valley were yielding millions of feet of timber at good prices and the little mills were busy turning out chair stock and the like. They carried a long list of charges to the 1906 legislature and demanded creation of a new state railroad commission with powers parallel to those of the Interstate Commerce Commission. They charged that freight rates were inequitable; that they couldn't get enough cars for their goods; that cars stood on sidings for days after they were loaded waiting to be taken away; that the locomotives couldn't handle the business; that the rails were so light they turned over under the weight of half a dozen cars, and that, since the locomotives couldn't haul a full car of grain, farmers had to buy in small lots. Whether the legislature was impressed with this indictment or not, it didn't create a commission.

Within six months the shippers formed the West River Lumbermen's Association for the specific purpose of carrying on the war, and their first act was to adopt a resolution charging that the railroad was "operated without proper regard to the business interests of the shippers along its line." An executive committee instructed to work for better service found plenty to do but not much to congratulate itself on.

Next the lumbermen went to the state railroad commission, which they had charged was powerless when they were trying to get a new one. In a lengthy petition they prayed for an order instructing the CV to revise freight rates downward, supply adequate motive power and rolling stock, build larger sidings and make the track safe in general. They alleged that five million feet of lumber stood beside the tracks waiting to be hauled away. They never filed this petition but took care that the CV learned of its existence.

A few weeks later they claimed a bloodless victory, saying that service had improved and that the CV had promised to repair the track. They congratulated themselves too soon, for the next time the legislature met they were at Montpelier declaring that the road was in "unsafe and unfit condition for transportation of freight and passengers." They were also still crying for lower lumber rates, a measure of which they got by bringing the Public Service Commission to Brattleboro for a hearing. Before the hearing opened the various attorneys went into conference and emerged with word that the CV would grant a reduction. At the same time roadbed repairs were promised; but if promises could have run the West River it would have outstripped the New York Central. Usually they resulted in a few new ties and rails but the rate of replacement never kept pace with deterioration.

Passengers were less articulate but they were sometimes found with

THREE CARS WOULD FIT ON PARK SIDING, NORTH OF TOWNSHEND,
BEFORE THE '27 FLOOD. OBJECT IN CENTER IS A BOX CAR

A TYPICAL WEST RIVER RR TRAIN IN THE MID-TWENTIES

THESE GASOLINE CARS BURNED SHORTLY AFTER THIS 1938 PICTURE

OLD 36
AT THE
TANK

the complainants, too. One of the things that wore their patience thin was the practice of carrying livestock in the passenger cars. One morning when a dozen or so rode into Brattleboro in a car with fourteen calves and two sheep their reactions made the daily paper's front page. The stock actually was in the express compartment, more or less divided from the rest of the car, but passengers said there was little difference for olfactory purposes.

The Brattleboro & Whitehall organization, which entertained fond hopes when it gave away its nominal ownership in return for broad gauge, also entered the battle. When the directors' free passes were not renewed in 1907 they set up a howl. The CV explained that a new state law forbade railroads' giving free tickets and passes, a practice which had become vicious, but the directors succeeded in claiming an exemption. Thereafter they rode when they chose until the same situation arose during World War I when the railroad was under government administration. The B&W attorney went to Washington and all but stopped the war as he toiled upward from dignitary to dignitary explaining that the passes were a term of the 1905 foreclosure agreement. At length the government had the CV pay $50, which was all the directors' transportation was considered worth, into the operating account and they rode free once more.

The string of protests reached a climax in 1919 with a day set aside for public indignation meetings along the line. At Williamsville, Newfane and Townshend, patrons gathered to announce that they could tolerate matters no longer. The well-worn complaint that lumber couldn't be shipped to market was aired and reinforced by others. Often no evening mail was received, they said, because the postoffices closed before the train arrived, loaded cars waited a week before they were picked up and thousands of ties were rotten. One lumber dealer claimed he was put out

36

of business because he couldn't get cars. Less than carload lots were picked up only on Fridays, shippers said, and only one car was provided. If the car was filled before it got to the end of the line nothing was taken at the rest of the stations. Sometimes shipments on the wrong end waited two or three Fridays.

The result of these meetings was more promises, but soon the B&W directors, their patience exhausted, went again to the courts. A lengthy bill of complaint listed numerous grievances, including abandonment of stations, and demanded that the CV live up to the foreclosure agreement of 1905 "to properly accommodate the freight and passenger business naturally coming to said road."

The CV replied that the service was adequate and that closing stations and handling less than carload lots only on Fridays did not violate the agreement. It also claimed that the West River line had been operated at an average annual loss of $20,000 since it was opened. This probably was not exaggeration. From 1922 until December 12, 1927, when the CV went into receivership, operating records were kept separately and showed the following deficits:

1922	$45,961.66	1925	42,020.50
1923	48,290.52	1926	42,676.16
1924	39,315.00	1927	50,465.07

In 1924 B&W stockholders met at Brattleboro for what amounted to their last annual meeting. The foreclosure agreement by which they received free transportation on annual meeting day ran out within the year and took off the holiday edge. They went home still protesting

ENGINE NO. 51
SETTLES FOR
A WINTER'S
NAP NEAR THE
MILL YARD IN
TOWNSHEND.

poor service and high freight rates and ordered the directors to forestall rumored removal of the thrice-a-week passenger train. (The directors failed.) Two years later the stockholders got their last 1 percent dividend, the first in fifteen years.

The flood of 1927 put an end to wrangling about the service. Running wild, West River tore out bridges, swept long sections of the roadbed away and left long stretches of track a twisted ribbon of steel. The Salmon Hole bridge and two smaller ones were destroyed and the track was buried deep under landslides in many places. The locomotive was snug in the Brattleboro roundhouse at the time, but thirteen boxcars were marooned, some of them overturned, at various stations until the next through train ran—four years later under new auspices. Until the reconstruction there was no service except from Brattleboro to Newfane and that only a locomotive's occasional trip with a car or two.

Its main line devastated by the 1927 flood, the CV showed little interest in repairing the West River branch. From time to time in the months after the flood, high officials appeared in Brattleboro on their way from washout to washout and were buttonholed by local newspapermen. They expressed concern for the thirteen stranded boxcars, but for nothing else between Brattleboro and South Londonderry, and were careful to give the impression that they never would.

For a year matters dragged on thus, and meanwhile the valley residents forgot all the hard things they had said about the railroad. Such service as it had given loomed large against none at all and they were not ready to relinquish it altogether. Somewhere the notion sprang up that the legislature, which had lent the St. Johnsbury & Lake Champlain $300,000 to augment its reconstruction funds, might be persuaded to endow the West River. Where the scheme originated is not known. CV officials had hinted that they would give the railroad to anybody who would fix it, and this may have planted the idea. Or it may have been conceived in the valley, or in some attorney's brain. At any rate, an understanding quietly sprouted that the CV would give the line back to local ownership if somebody would repair it. A parallel understanding was that the state treasury should be the "somebody." Then the CV filed a petition for abandonment with the Interstate Commerce Commission.

In the last months of 1928 the state loan scheme reached the proportions of a movement. Up and down the valley it was embraced like a new way to salvation, and everybody began to persuade everybody else that it was a most practical project. With something of the unquenchable optimism that imbued the original promoters, the loan proponents got out their pencils and proved that it was a practical proposition. They said

$200,000 would be more than enough to repair and equip the line and there was plenty of business for it. They claimed the CV had created a deficit on paper by stocking the branch with worn-out, totally depreciated equipment and then charging high prices against it. This argument was buttressed by a plan to operate a non-union road with lower wages, and altogether annual net operating profit was conservatively estimated at $13,000.

In this frame of mind they went to the 1929 legislature and were given a hearing. A long line of witnesses appeared and unfolded a story of a valley facing ruin for want of a railroad. Some told of the innumerable carloads of this and that waiting to be shipped out and others said the valley would suffer a 50 percent drop in property appraisal, yea, even be totally depopulated, without the railroad. There was no formal opposition and only scattered counsel that $200,000 might produce more lasting benefit if invested in the highway.

Without a dissent the house passed the bill, while the senate sent it on for the governor's signature by a vote of twenty-five to four. The CV turned the road back to a directorate of local residents and in the summer of 1930, after long delay over legal technicalities, it was rebuilt.

The CV made the new owners a present of some discarded rolling stock and for $14,000 they bought a $28,000 locomotive built for plantation use but never taken out of the shop. On February 1, 1934, the 295 curves and the handful of straightaways which added up to 36 miles bore their first regular train in more than four years. There was no formal celebration, but here and there little knots of onlookers gathered and a few passengers climbed aboard. The schedule called for one trip to Brattleboro and back each day, as a mixed train four days a week and as a passenger on Wednesdays and Saturdays.

Weeks wore on and the glowing predictions lavished on the legislature went consistently unsupported. Freight shipments were few and passengers fewer. Whether the service was better or worse than that of the CV was not recorded, for no one seemed to notice. The train could have been tied up a week without anyone's missing it. In the fall regular trips were abandoned. The railroad contracted with a motor truck operator to carry its mail and occasional boxes of freight, and put the locomotive in storage.

The spring of 1933 brought on the scene one James G. Ashley, a mechanic from Greenfield, Massachusetts, who took a twenty-five year lease, was persuaded to part with $1,500, and announced he would put new life on the rusting rails. With a railroad itch in his blood, plenty of vigor and a lot of ideas, Ashley proceeded to lose his shirt.

First he bought a little gasoline-powered unit with a passenger car trailer discarded by the Hoosac Tunnel & Wilmington Railroad and launched regular service. Then he picked up a steam locomotive, the *H. H. Paine,* tossed on the scrap heap when the Woodstock Railroad was abandoned. With these he was ready for business—the gasoline outfit for light loads and the locomotive for heavy ones when there were any.

As soon as Ashley was ready for business on a big scale his reverses started. The *H. H. Paine* proved unsuited to the tortuous track and, after a maiden trip in which it was lucky to get up to South Londonderry, never traveled again until it was cut up for scrap and hauled away. The gasoline unit ran more or less successfully through the summer. Strangely enough, it frequently hauled passengers and Ashley did nothing to discourage them. He cut fares to two cents a mile long before the I.C.C. made the big railroads do likewise, and stopped anywhere for anybody who stood by the track and held up a hand. A winter of moderate snows was too much for the outfit, however, and before long Ashley was making trips only when the weather was right.

Next he bought a secondhand combination gasoline unit-and-passenger car from the Lehigh Valley but it was unaccustomed to steep grades and languished on the hills. Ultimately Ashley put a new engine in it and made it a serviceable contraption for passenger traffic, but by that time travelers had learned better than to depend on the railroad.

Meanwhile the first gasoline outfit caught fire and was destroyed. Just as it was pulling into West Dummerston flames shot out when the engine back-fired and in an instant the entire car was afire. The crew of two and the two passengers leaped to safety, the latter with just time to grab their luggage.

That was in May, 1934. At that time Ashley hadn't got his second gasoline car in good order and through the summer the rails bore few loads. When he had large freight shipments, which wasn't often, he used the lessors' engine; and when he didn't, he carried mail and smaller lots with a truck. By October he conceded that the traffic wouldn't support a steam locomotive and bought a third gasoline car, this one a sturdy machine capable of hauling a loaded freight car. It had seen service on the Boston & Maine.

It wasn't, however, equal to winter on the West River line and in a couple of months service was suspended again. Ashley gave up all hope of regular passenger trips and bought himself a bus.

Came the spring of 1935 and the warm sun freed the train from the snowdrifts which had held it at Jamaica all winter, but it never saw much service. Business had all but evaporated and an occasional car of granite turned out by the West Dummerston quarry constituted the major share of the traffic. The track, which had been a long way from good condition when Ashley took it over, was disintegrating, too. Bushes grew into the right of way and weeds obscured the rails. Ties rotted away and toward the last, Ashley cut down the old telegraph poles, squared them by hand and shoved them under the rails. After washouts he propped the track up with stones, fallen trees and old timbers.

His train and track crew dwindled away also until he was running a one-man railroad. When an assistant was needed, Mrs. Ashley was it. If

CLEARING THE TRACK IN THE LAST DAYS OF THE RAILROAD

a car had to be switched or a crossing flagged, Ashley summoned her from home to serve as an engineer while he turned brakeman.

With matters thus the lessors decided to cut the railroad's dying agony short. Early in 1936 they petitioned the Interstate Commerce Commission to abandon it and the state, which had taken the capital stock as security on its $200,000 loan, foreclosed. The next fall it was torn up. The rails north of West Dummerston, rolling stock and most of the bridges went to a salvage company. The $14,000 locomotive was sold to a southern line for $2,500. In order that West Dummerston might keep its quarry open if possible, the six miles to Brattleboro were left and sold to the quarry at less than junk price on easy terms. Fixtures from the old stations went at public auction and the stations themselves were put to a variety of uses. Some became dwellings and one a real estate agent's office. The West Dummerston bridge was left for the convenience of the quarry, while that over the Salmon Hole was reserved for possible highway use. But in World War II it was taken down for scrap iron.

The 6-mile section to the quarry lasted two years and ran true to form, ending in a tangle. It was in poor shape when the company, Vermont White Granite Quarries, Incorporated, took it over and it grew steadily worse. Scant use was made of it and then in the fall of 1938 came the flood and hurricane, which did further damage. At this point the company sold it for junk, reserving a bridge at the north end which gave easy access to the highway and which in the meantime had been planked to carry trucks.

When a check to discharge the mortgage arrived in Montpelier a howl arose under the golden dome of the capitol. The state sold the line to the company for $5,000 when it could have got $6,000 cash as junk, just to help the community to retain an industry and not to finance anyone's speculation, state officials declared. The price of scrap had risen meanwhile and the quarry company, controlled by Earl Baldwin of Brattleboro, had sold it for $7,000 and kept the bridge in the bargain. Conferences ensued and the matter was settled with the state's getting $6,000, the price it was offered in the first place, and the bridge. In the summer of 1939 the last rails were removed. Thus Baldwin became probably the only man to turn a dollar out of a $600,000 railroad.

Altogether, the state got some $30,000 salvage and in addition the right of way where the abutting landowners didn't succeed in proving a better claim. One section of the old roadbed has been used for a highway.

Thus ignominiously ended the railroad's fifty-six-year career. Viewed dispassionately, it was a doubtful asset at best and during its life consumed more than $300,000 of public funds and broke Ashley, besides whatever burden it was to the Central Vermont. Nevertheless, up and down the valley its loss is still mentioned in a tone of regret.

"Business isn't what it was when we had the railroad," many persons say, vaguely connecting it with lost glories. In its early days it was a useful if not faithful servant and most persons in the valley believe its contributions to the convenience of living outweighed, in some measure, its unreliability and its subsidy. Had not times changed it might have continued indefinitely as a "jerk-line" railroad. But with high-powered motors and improved highways the valley found it could get along better without a railroad, as it was finally willing to admit. Under such conditions a railroad was an expensive indulgence.

WILLIAMSVILLE STATION, NOW THE PROPERTY OF ROBERT L. CROWELL, HAS
BEEN MOVED AROUND THE CORNER AND UP THE HILL TO MAKE WAY FOR
ROUTE 30 CONSTRUCTION AND A NEW HIGHWAY BRIDGE ON THE SITE OF THE
WEST RIVER RR's ROCK RIVER SPAN SHOWN IN THE 1911 SCENE ABOVE.

NO MORE DO NEWFANE LADIES WAIT TRACKSIDE–TO
FLAG DOWN "THE BULL OF THE WOODS?" . . . TO GRAB
THE MAIL? . . . TO HAND UP THE ENGINEER'S LUNCH? THE
DATE OF THIS BUCOLIC SCENE IS UNKNOWN.

THE END